Cody's Snake Tale

Wendy Graham
Illustrated by Ben O'Hagan

Contents

Chapter 1
A Desert Vacation

Cody and Ben Lopez unpacked their bags in the cabin. They'd just started their vacation, but Cody wasn't happy. The problem wasn't the hiking and exploring. He loved the outdoors, and he had brought his sketch pad. He wanted to draw the plants and animals they saw. The problem wasn't the company. He was with his brother Ben and their dad. That was fine.

The problem was the place Dad had chosen for their vacation—the Sonoran desert in southwestern Arizona. It was home to Cody's biggest fear—snakes!

"Ben," Cody began, "did you know this place has snakes? Even rattlesnakes!"

"Cool," said Ben. "I hope we see some."
Suddenly, he shouted, "There's one!"

Cody leaped back.

"There, in the picture on the wall," Ben
said, laughing.

It wasn't funny to Cody. He had a little knot of fear in his stomach that wouldn't go away. He didn't mind the other creatures of the desert—scorpions, tarantulas, lizards, toads. But snakes were a different matter. Snakes were his worst nightmare.

When everyone had unpacked, the family set off on their first hike.

"I wish we'd gone somewhere with a skateboard ramp," Cody muttered.

"Come on, now, Cody," Dad said. "You'll have fun. We'll see wild animals, like rabbits, coyotes, and javelinas. There are all kinds of mammals in the desert. Not to mention reptiles and amphibians."

"What's the difference between reptiles and amphibians?" asked Ben. "Aren't they the same kind of animal?"

Dad shook his head. "Amphibians go through a process called *metamorphosis*. When baby amphibians hatch from their eggs, they live in water and breathe through gills, like fish. When the babies grow up, they grow lungs and move onto the land."

"Right," said Ben.

"But baby reptiles look like their parents when they hatch, except the babies are smaller. They breathe air from the minute they come out of their eggs. Did you know snakes are a kind of reptile?"

"Okay, Dad, switch off," Cody said. "You sound like some guy on *Quiz of the Century.*"

"Don't be rude, son," Dad said.

Cody was quiet, but only for a moment. "Well, don't go on about snakes," he said. "I hate snakes, so I don't like talking about them." He ran a little way ahead of the others, embarrassed by his outburst.

Chapter 2
Desert Creatures

As he walked on, Cody heard a rustling sound in the bushes nearby. He jumped with fright and froze. Was it a snake? He looked around, listening. Then he ran back to the others. "I heard a noise over there," he said, pointing.

"Hey, look!" Ben gasped.

The rustling became louder as two javelinas appeared. They looked like hairy brown pigs.

"Sshhh," Dad said. "Let's stop and watch them for a while. Keep quiet."

They stood watching the animals from a distance. Ben took some photos. When

the javelinas moved away, the family took another path.

Ben jumped with excitement. "Yay! I want to see some more wild animals. Hey, Cody, we might see some gila monsters—great big poisonous lizards. Some are as long as a cat!"

While Cody was looking the other way, Ben moved behind him. Suddenly he jumped onto Cody's back. Cody yelled in fright. Then he realized it was only Ben playing a trick.

12

"You rat!" Cody said.

"Boys, boys," their dad said. "Behave yourselves. Hey, look, I've found something here."

The boys hurried to have a look. It was the old outer skin of a cicada.

"Isn't that neat?" Dad said. "Cicadas go through metamorphosis, too. When they hatch from their eggs, they don't have wings. They live underground. When they come out of the ground, they shed their skin. Underneath their old skin, they've grown wings. This is the old skin, here."

"Boring," sang Ben, in a sing-song voice. "I want to see something scary. Like a snake!"

Cody swallowed.

They spent the rest of the day exploring. Everyone took turns posing for photos in front of different kinds of cactus. Ben saw a gila monster. But it was only a quick glimpse of its spotted back before it returned underground.

That night in their cabin, Cody checked that the outer doors were tightly closed.

"What's the matter, Cody?" asked Ben. "Scared of a little scorpion getting into your bed?"

Cody didn't answer. Scorpions, huh! There was only one thing he was afraid might get inside. It had five letters and started with S.

Chapter 3
Shedding Skins

The following day, the family hiked near some low hills. Something in the bushes caught Ben's eye. He gasped, then shouted, "Stop!" Everyone stopped. Ben pointed with his stick. "Snake!" he yelled.

"Sure, Ben," said Cody, pretending he wasn't afraid. "I'm not falling for that trick again!"

"I'm not joking!" Ben replied.

Their father pointed his binoculars at the shape in the distance. "It's okay," he said. "It's not a snake. It's a snake *skin*. Let's have a look."

It was an entire rattlesnake skin, from head to tail.

"Wow," Cody said, no longer afraid now that he knew it was only a skin. He stepped closer and looked at it. The patterns on the skin were amazing. They were better than anything he could ever draw. "Why do snakes shed their skin?" he asked his dad.

"It's part of the growing process," Dad replied. "When the snake gets too large for

its skin, it sheds the old skin. A new, larger skin is underneath."

Cody was curious. "Well, how come other animals don't shed their skins, too?"

Ben knew a little more than Cody. "Some do," Ben said. "Some lizards shed their skins in one piece, like snakes. Alligators and turtles shed their skin, too. But they don't shed their whole skin at once. They shed small patches of skin all the time."

"Let's get going, guys," Dad said.

Everyone took long drinks of water, and continued the hike. Cody lingered a minute, looking back at the snake skin. He wanted to stay and look at it a little longer.

Chapter 4
Around the Campfire

That evening the boys and their dad sat around the campfire. The sky was black, dotted with thousands of diamond-bright stars. A trail guide named Zac stopped by the campfire.

Cody and Ben were holding some hot dogs over the fire on long sticks. Cody spoke to Zac. "Excuse me," he said. "Do you know anything about rattlesnakes?" Cody wasn't sure why he needed to know more. He just knew that he got more interested in snakes when he saw the snake skin.

"Sure," Zac said. "What do you want to know?"

"Well," Cody said, "what makes the rattling sound?"

Cody's question was interrupted by music from a guitar. It was a woman from the group at a nearby campfire. Soon, Dad

and Ben were listening to her play and singing along. But not Cody. He was more interested in talking about the rattlesnake. "Zac, what causes the rattling sound?" he repeated.

"A rattler's tail has lots of little segments on the end. When the snake is scared, it shakes its tail. The rattling sound is made when the segments of the rattle click against each other." Zac listened to the music and snapped his fingers in time with the beat.

Ben interrupted. "You know, a few days ago, Cody was terrified of snakes, and now he can't stop talking about them."

"I wasn't afraid of snakes," Cody said. "I was afraid of getting bitten by one, that's all."

"Well, as long as we respect them and take precautions, that isn't likely," Zac said. He joined the others in clapping for the guitarist as the music faded.

Later, back in their cabin, Cody got out his sketch pad and pencils. He drew a large rattlesnake. He copied the pattern of its scales from the picture on the wall, getting each detail perfect.

That night, Cody fell asleep thinking about snakes. Maybe they weren't so bad after all, but he still hoped he never had to get close to one!

Chapter 5
The Desert Museum

In the morning, Cody woke up feeling disappointed. This was their last day. They all packed their bags.

"I have a surprise for you," said Dad. "Before we leave, we're going to visit the desert museum. We'll watch the live reptile presentation."

Cody had mixed feelings about seeing the live reptiles. He was scared, but also fascinated. They entered the museum and the presentation began. The snake handler lifted a snake from a bag. "This is a harmless fellow," she said. "He's a common king snake." She brought the snake closer to Cody. He stepped back.

"It's okay," the handler said to Cody.
"Here, feel the snake's skin. You'll be
surprised."

Cody didn't want to touch the snake,
but everyone was watching. Slowly, he

reached out and touched its back. "Wow," Cody said. "I thought it would be slimy, but it's not. It feels dry."

The snake didn't seem to mind Cody touching it. Cody's confidence grew. He stroked his hand along the snake's curved back. He admired its coloring and pattern. It was dark brown, almost black, with narrow bands of white around its body. It moved slowly and calmly in the handler's grasp. Ben took a photo of Cody, smiling, with his hand on the snake.

Soon the handler put the king snake back in its bag. Then she showed a different snake. "Now, this guy here," she said, "is not so gentle. This is a rattlesnake."

Excitement took over Cody as his eyes followed it. It was also a beautiful creature, he realized. He noticed its smoothness and shape, the patterned markings, its banded tail and rattle.

The snake handler told about the rattlesnake. Cody listened carefully.

"People most often see rattlesnakes in the wild in spring, summer, and fall," she said. "Did you know that even baby rattlesnakes are poisonous?"

"Wow," gasped Ben. "They must be dangerous!"

"Yes, they can be," replied the handler. "But when a rattlesnake bites, it's usually for a reason—a person tries to touch it, or steps on it by accident. As long as you look where you're walking and stay clear if you do see a rattlesnake, you'll be pretty safe." She smiled. "In fact, rattlesnakes are more scared of

people than we are of them!"

Ben nudged Cody. "I bet you're still afraid of the snake," he whispered.

"No, I'm not," Cody whispered back. He realized that he wasn't afraid anymore.

A happy excitement took hold of him. He really had touched a live snake! And seen a real rattler! Awesome!

"All right, boys, time to leave," Dad said.

"Oh, do we have to?" Cody asked.

As they moved toward the exit, Cody nudged his father. "Hey, Dad, I had the best time," he said. "Can we come here again next vacation?"

Rattlesnakes

Rattlesnakes are reptiles. Like other reptiles, such as lizards and turtles, they have scales and are cold-blooded. Most reptiles lay eggs, but rattlesnakes do not.

When a baby rattlesnake is born, it doesn't have a rattle on its tail. As the rattlesnake grows, it sheds its skin from time to time. There is new skin underneath. Every time a rattlesnake sheds its skin, a section of its rattle grows.

Rattlesnakes use their rattles to warn predators to stay away.

Think About the Story

In *Cody's Snake Tale*, Cody goes hiking in the Sonoran desert with his family. Cody is frightened of snakes. Think about the questions below.

- What animals does Cody see in the desert?
- What does Dad tell Cody and Ben about cicadas?
- What does Cody learn about snakes during his trip? How does this help him overcome his fear?

To learn more about life cycles of animals, read the books below.

SUGGESTED READING
Windows on Literacy
The Amazing Silkworm
Groups of Animals

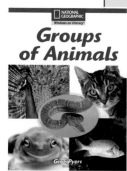